GAME DAY

Jump Ball!

You Can Play Basketball

by Nick Fauchald ✳ illustrated by Bill Dickson

Thanks to our advisers for their expertise, research, and advice:

Wendy Frappier, Ph.D.
Assistant Professor, Health and Physical Education Department
Minnesota State University
Moorhead, Minnesota

Susan Kesselring, M.A., Literacy Educator
Rosemount-Apple Valley-Eagan (Minnesota) School District

PICTURE WINDOW BOOKS
Minneapolis, Minnesota

Managing Editor: Bob Temple
Creative Director: Terri Foley
Editor: Brenda Haugen
Editorial Adviser: Andrea Cascardi
Copy Editor: Sue Gregson
Designer: Nathan Gassman
Page production: Picture Window Books
The illustrations in this book are watercolor.

Picture Window Books
5115 Excelsior Boulevard
Suite 232
Minneapolis, MN 55416
1-877-845-8392
www.picturewindowbooks.com

Printed in the United States of America.

Library of Congress Cataloging-in-Publication Data
Fauchald, Nick.
Jump Ball!: You can play basketball / written by Nick
Fauchald ; illustrated by Bill Dickson.
p. cm. — (Game day)
Includes bibliographical references (p.   ) and index.
Summary: A brief introduction to the game
of basketball as intended to be played by children.
ISBN 1-4048-0261-4 (lib. bdg.)
1. Basketball Juvenile literature. [1. Basketball.]
I. Dickson, Bill, 1949- ill. II. Title.
GV885.1 .F38 2004
796.323—dc22   2003019637

Basketball is a fast and exciting sport to play and watch. You can play it indoors or outdoors. All you need is a hoop, a basketball, and some friends. A team scores by shooting the basketball through the other team's hoop. The team with the most points at the end of the game wins!

Your team, the Wizards, is playing the Slammers today. You bring your tennis shoes to the court and stretch your muscles. Then the Wizards practice passing and shooting.

Basketball is played on a rectangular court with a hoop at each end. Each team has five players on the court at a time.

5

Game time! The two teams meet in the middle of the court for the jump ball. The referee tosses the ball up in the air between two players—one from each team.

The two players jump and try to tap the ball to their teammates. The Wizards grab the ball first. Patrick dribbles it toward the Slammers' basket.

A player moves the ball up and down the court by bouncing it with one hand. This is called dribbling. You also can move the ball by passing it to a teammate.

7

Patrick passes the ball to Julie.
The other Wizards move around
to get open for a pass.

The team with the ball is on offense. The other team is on defense. The team on defense guards the players on offense to keep them from scoring. The best way to play defense is by staying between the person you are guarding and the basket.

Julie dribbles, stops, and passes the ball to you.

You turn toward the basket and shoot.

The ball bounces off the rim, and a Slammer grabs it. You missed, but it was a good try.

Once you stop dribbling the ball, you have to pass it or shoot it. If you start dribbling again, it is called a double dribble. If you move more than one of your feet while holding the ball, it is called traveling. When you do either of these, the other team gets the ball.

11

Now the Slammers have the ball. The player you are guarding dribbles closer and closer to the basket.

As she's dribbling, you reach out and knock the ball away.

When you play defense, you can steal the ball from the player who is dribbling. Make sure you don't trip or push the other player, or the referee will call a foul.

You run near the basket and get open for a pass.

Lisa sees you and passes the ball right into your hands.

You turn toward the basket and shoot.

The ball swooshes through the hoop.
Two points for the Wizards!

A basket is usually
worth two points.
A free throw is
worth one point.
Bouncing the ball
off the backboard
sometimes can help
you make a shot.

The Slammers move the ball
up the court and make a basket.
There is less than one minute left
in the first quarter.

Carlos dribbles around a Slammer
and looks for someone to pass to
near the basket.

Practice dribbling with your left hand and with your right hand. Try to keep your head up. By looking ahead, you can see if your teammates are open for a pass.

Carlos sees you under the basket. He throws the ball toward you. The seconds tick off the clock—five, four, three. You jump up, catch the ball, and shoot. Two seconds. One second.

The ball drops through the hoop! That's the end of the first quarter, but there's lots more basketball to be played.

Basketball games usually are divided into four quarters.

21

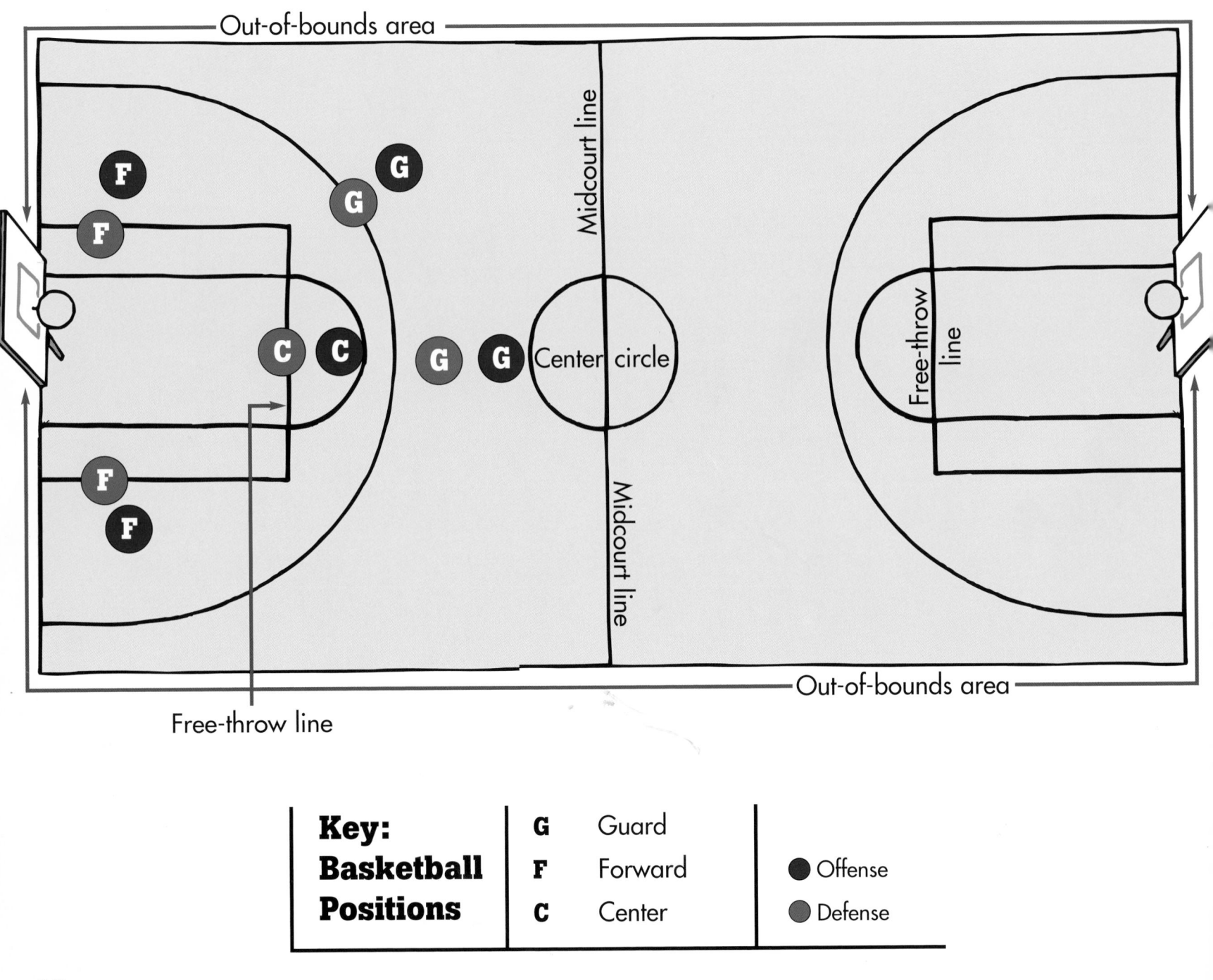

Out-of-bounds area

Midcourt line

Center circle

Free-throw line

Midcourt line

Out-of-bounds area

Free-throw line

Key:	G	Guard	
Basketball	F	Forward	● Offense
Positions	C	Center	● Defense

Fun Facts

 Dr. James Naismith invented basketball in 1891 when he was a teacher at the YMCA in Springfield, Massachusetts. He used two peach baskets as hoops, and the backboards were made of wire. People climbed a ladder to get the ball after it landed in the basket. No one had yet thought of cutting the bottoms out of the baskets!

 In 1949, the National Basketball Association (NBA) was formed when two leagues, the Basketball Association of America and the National Basketball League, combined.

In 1962, Philadelphia 76ers center Wilt Chamberlain scored 100 points in one game—the most ever scored in an NBA game.

Kareem Abdul-Jabbar is the NBA's all-time leading scorer. He scored a total of 38,387 points in 20 seasons.

Glossary

defense—the team that does not have the ball. The defense tries to keep the other team from scoring.

dribble—to bounce the ball with one hand

foul—when a player pushes, trips, or grabs a player on the other team

free throw—a free shot taken from the free-throw line after a foul

offense—the team that has the ball. The offense tries to score points.

pass—to throw or bounce the ball to a teammate

steal—to take the ball away from the other team

traveling—moving more than one foot while holding the basketball

To Learn More

At the Library

Eule, Brian. *Basketball for Fun.* Minneapolis: Compass Point Books, 2003.

Gibbons, Gail. *My Basketball Book.* New York: HarperCollins Publishers, 2000.

Weatherspoon, Teresa. *Teresa Weatherspoon's Basketball for Girls.* New York: John Wiley & Sons, Inc., 1999.

Zeltwanger, Paul E. *Basketball Is My Game: How I Learned to Love the Sport.* Cincinnati: SportsKid, 2001.

On the Web

Fact Hound
Fact Hound offers a safe, fun way to find Web sites related to this book.
All of the sites on Fact Hound have been researched by our staff.
http://www.facthound.com

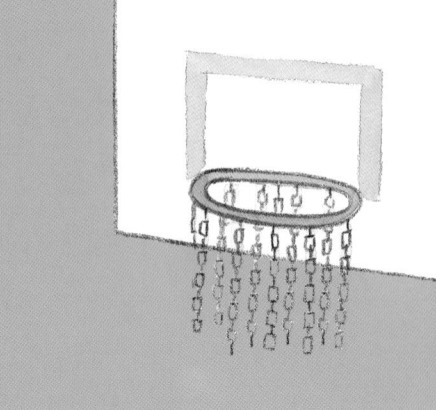

1. Visit the Fact Hound home page.

2. Enter a search word related to this book, or type in this special code:1404802614.

3. Click on the FETCH IT button.

Your trusty Fact Hound will fetch the best sites for you!

Index